MY LIFE

My Growing Body

WRITTEN BY C.J. POLIN
ILLUSTRATED BY RYAN WHEATCROFT

PowerKiDS press
New York

Published in 2023 by The Rosen Publishing Group, Inc.
29 East 21st Street, New York, NY 10010

Editors: Sarah Peutrill and Sarah Ridley
Design: Anthony Hannant (Little Red Ant)

Cataloging-in-Publication Data

Names: Polin, C.J. | Wheatcroft, Ryan, illustrator.
Title: My growing body / by C.J. Polin, illustrated by Ryan Wheatcroft.
Description: New York : Powerkids Press, 2023. | Series: My life | Includes glossary and index.
Identifiers: ISBN 9781725338210 (pbk.) | ISBN 9781725338234 (library bound) | ISBN 9781725338227 (6pack) | ISBN 9781725338241 (ebook)
Subjects: LCSH: Life cycle, Human--Juvenile literature. | Children--Growth--Juvenile literature. | Developmental biology--Juvenile literature.
Classification: LCC QP83.8 P655 2023 | DDC 612.6--dc23

Manufactured in the United States of America

CPSIA Compliance Information: Batch #CSPK23. For further information contact Rosen Publishing, New York, New York at 1-800-237-9932.

Find us on

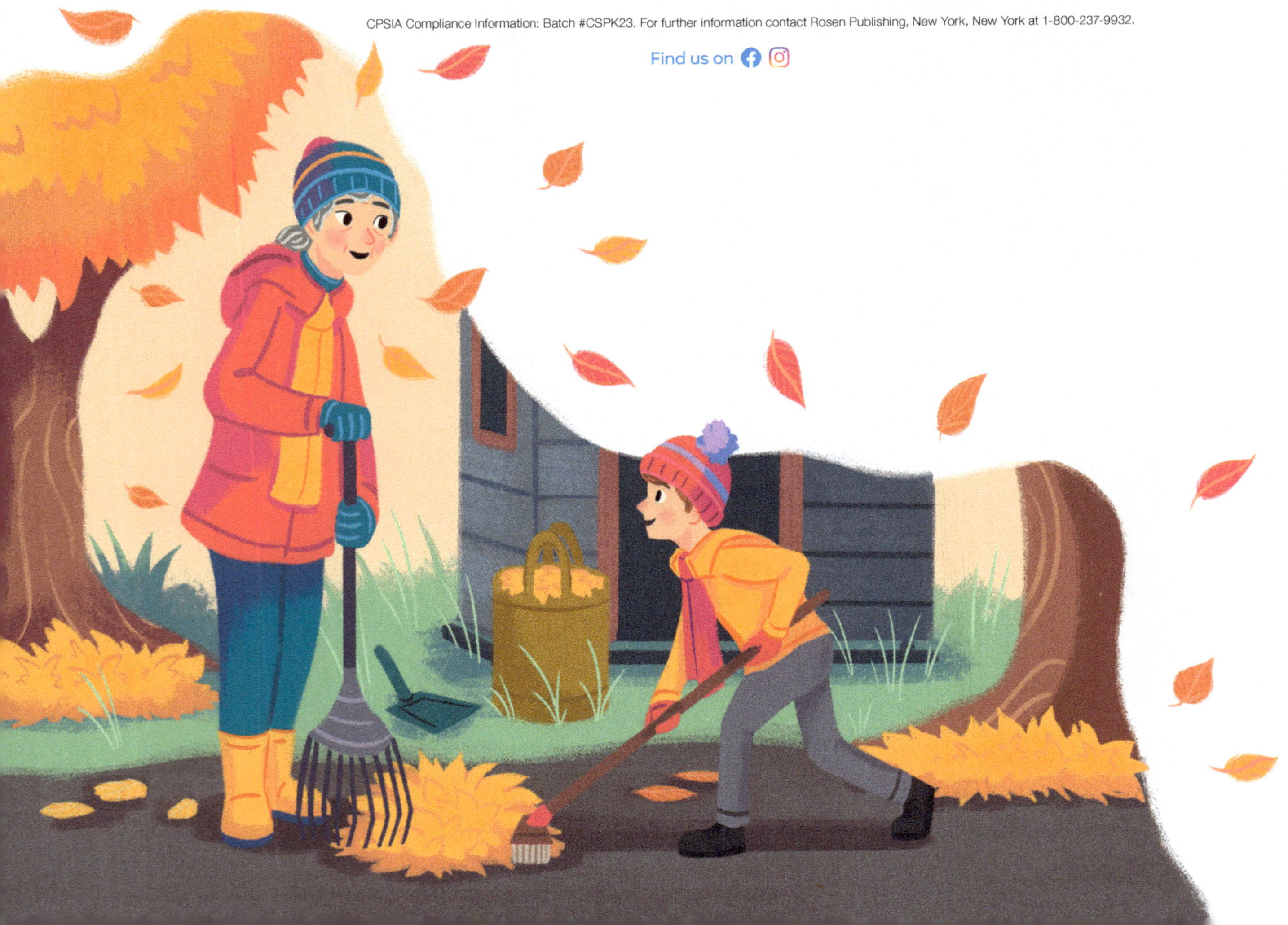

CONTENTS

OUR LIFE CYCLE

What is always changing but we hardly ever notice? It's us! We are born and we grow from children into adults, then we may have our own children. We keep growing older and, in the end, we die. These changes are the life cycle of a human being.

These pictures show some of the stages of the human life cycle.

Growing

When you are a child, you grow a lot. You can see this when your feet get too big for your shoes or when you look at photos of when you were younger. Childhood is the years between when you are born and when you have finished growing and can look after yourself, usually at about the age of 18. Then you are an adult, but you still continue to change.

Some things about you are the same as some other people–the color of your eyes, for example, or that you like swimming. But no one else in the entire world is exactly like you. You have your own look and personality. You even grow and change a little differently than everyone else. There are millions of people in the world, and each of us is unique.

Today, people in countries such as the United States and Canada often live to the age of 80 or even older. But 200 years ago, people only expected to live to about the age of 40.

HOW YOUR BODY GROWS

Your body is made up of lots of tiny building blocks called cells. Lots of different types of body cells exist inside your body. Similar cells group together to form different parts of your body, such as your muscles or your blood. During your childhood, your body makes more and more cells as it grows and grows and grows!

Your Skeleton

Your skeleton is made of bone and a flexible body tissue called cartilage. When you were born, your skeleton had about 300 parts, most of which were made of cartilage.

Gradually, some of the cartilage turned into strong bone and some of the bones joined together. By the time you become an adult, your skeleton will contain 206 bones.

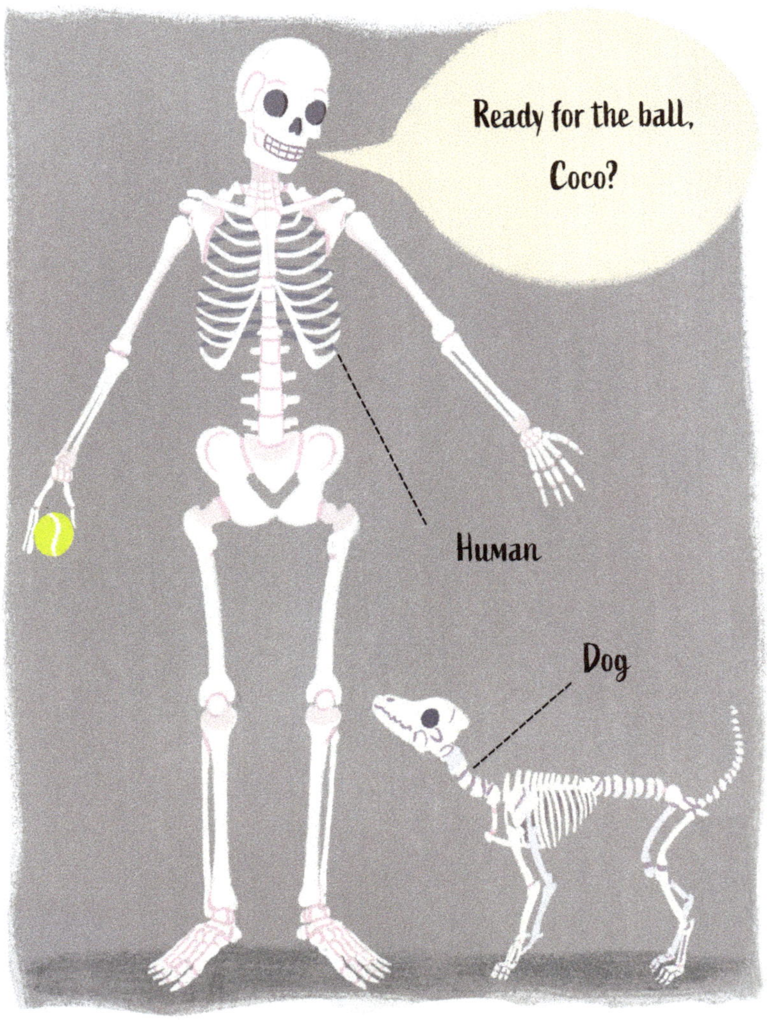

Skeletons of a human and a dog. Most people reach adult height between the ages of 17 and 25.

A Healthy Body

Your body needs certain things to help it grow and work properly. Exercise makes your bones and muscles stronger and helps your heart and lungs work at their best. Different foods give your body energy, help it grow and repair itself, and protect it from certain illnesses. Sleep lets your body grow, repair itself, and fight off illnesses.

?

What kinds of food help keep your body healthy?

In order to kick a ball, your brain and your body need to work together. Tara's little brother is learning how to do this.

Brain Power

As your body grows, your brain also learns new things. You take in information through the five senses: seeing, hearing, touching, smelling, and tasting. The cells in your brain sort the information so you can remember it. Your brain and your body also learn to work together so you can walk, talk, write your name, ride a bike, and do lots of other activities. Your brain needs sleep to allow you to remember what you have learned.

BABIES

You grew inside your mother's womb for nine months before you were born. When you are a baby, you grow and learn more quickly than at any other time in your life. It might seem that a baby doesn't do much, but all the time, the baby is taking in new information. That can be tiring!

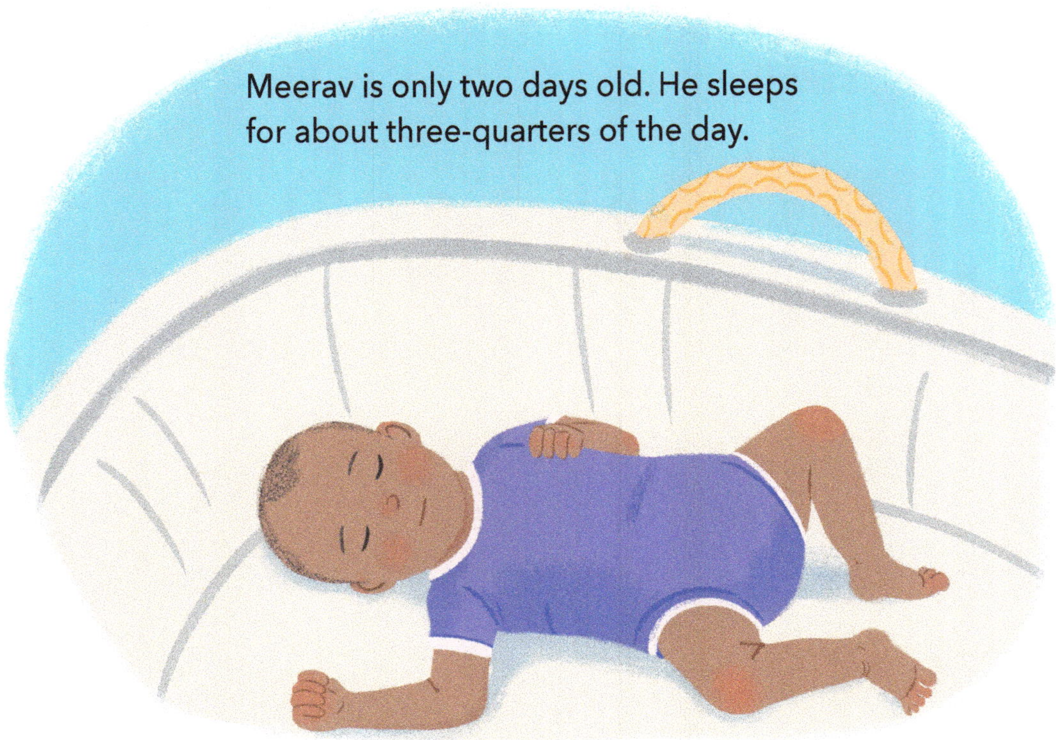

Newborn Baby

When you were a baby, you needed a lot of looking after. You depended on others for everything. Crying was your main way of telling people what you needed. You cried when you were hungry or cold, or needed a clean diaper.

Basic Skills

As you grew, you learned to do more. You probably gave your first real smile when you were about six weeks old. You made different sounds, such as gurgling and cooing. After about six months, your baby teeth started coming through so you could eat mashed up food.

Maya has learned to move her arms and legs together, so she can crawl across the floor.

First Year

As you grew older, you became bigger and stronger. Between six months and one year, most babies learn to sit up and then crawl. By your first birthday, you were about three times bigger than when you were born.

Children, especially babies, often learn by copying. Try making faces at a baby and see what happens.

TODDLERS

By the age of one-and-a-half, most children have learned to walk. This marks the beginning of the toddler stage. You probably said your first few words at about this age too. Walking and talking are important milestones in growing up.

Saraya has just started walking on her own. Very young children like Saraya find it difficult to balance, which is why they're called "toddlers."

Growing and Learning

A toddler's body continues growing taller. Moving around helps muscles grow stronger. As a toddler, you learned by playing with adults and older children. You learned about colors, shapes, and counting. You may have enjoyed songs and nursery rhymes. Toddlers don't understand about sharing and taking turns. You probably played alongside other children instead of playing with them.

Toddlers don't know that some things could be dangerous, such as hot pans or busy roads, so they must be watched carefully and told about the dangers.

Lewis and Rory explore the sounds the bells make. They are more interested in the bells than in playing together.

Learning Control

Did you have tantrums when you were a toddler? Toddlers have to learn how to cope with lots of new experiences and feelings–and it isn't easy! As you learned to talk, you were able to say what you wanted and sometimes that led to clashes with your parent or caregiver. Gradually children learn to manage their feelings rather than have a tantrum. Another thing you learned to control was your pee and poo so you could use the toilet. This often happens at the end of the toddler stage, between the ages of two and three.

EARLY CHILDHOOD

As you grew out of the toddler stage at about the age of three, you became more aware of the world around you. Young children often ask lots of questions because they are curious about everything.

Making Friends

Between the ages of about three and five, you started to think a bit less about yourself and more about other people. You enjoyed playing with other children and started to choose your own friends. You also began to learn that it's kinder to share and take turns.

Jason and his friend Freya learn about the world through pretend play.

New Skills

At this age, you were gaining better control of your body. Difficult movements became possible, such as hopping on one leg. Your hands and eyes started working together for activities such as throwing and catching. Small movements, such as gripping a pencil correctly, became possible as well.

Leo has learned to hold his pencil correctly. It is much easier to draw pictures now.

At around three or four years old, children often learn to sing the alphabet, identify letters, and learn letter sounds. They are getting ready for reading.

MIDDLE YEARS

You are probably now in the middle years of childhood, between the ages of about six and twelve. How have you changed since you were a baby? You can do all sorts of things–read a book, write, draw, run, and jump. And you are much taller, although you still have more growing to do.

Fatima already has some of her adult teeth. She also has some gaps and a wobbly tooth that will come out soon.

Teeth

Another thing that's changing is your teeth! Your baby teeth are coming out and your adult teeth are coming through. You'll keep these adult teeth for the rest of your life, so look after them.

Thinking for Yourself

You're now better able to understand right and wrong, and you're becoming more responsible. You can get yourself ready for school every day and help around the house and do homework without being reminded. You might also start thinking into the future by, for example, saving up your money to buy something special.

Kiki, Will, and their friends meet at the park nearly every Saturday. They like having fun together.

?

How much exercise do you get? Children should exercise for an hour or more a day.

Alicia didn't know much about music until she tried playing a guitar at school. Now she takes lessons and really enjoys it.

Exploring

You're learning to read and write well, ride a bike, tell the time, play sports–lots of things you couldn't do before. You probably like spending more time with your friends. This is a good time to try new activities to find what you are good at or enjoy. Exploring new things makes you feel good about yourself.

TEENAGE YEARS

Puberty is the stage of life when your body gets ready to become an adult. You may have a growth spurt and notice that your body is changing fast. Your feelings change too.

During puberty, your body works hard dealing with all of the changes, so it needs lots of sleep.

Hormones

Different people start puberty at different ages, but it's usually between the ages of 10 and 14. During puberty, chemicals in your body called hormones make lots of changes happen. Girls have female hormones, and boys have male hormones. Your hormones will cause hair to grow under your arms and between your legs. You'll also sweat more, so it is good to shower every day and start using deodorant to help you smell fresh.

Arthur is 15 years old. He's grown 1 foot (30 cm) since he was 12. You will go through a growth spurt during puberty.

Mood Swings

Life can seem confusing when you're going through puberty. You're not a child or an adult. One minute you feel happy and lively, then you feel down in the dumps. These mood swings are part of the enormous changes that you go through during puberty.

Ellie doesn't always like what she sees in the mirror. She has good days and bad days.

Emotions

As you go through puberty, you may change how you feel about people. You may start thinking about certain people in a romantic way. You might feel attracted to people. These feelings are a normal part of growing up.

Your body belongs to you. It is up to you whether you are hugged, tickled, or touched. It is not OK for someone to ask you to show them your private parts (the parts covered by underwear) or to ask you to touch their private parts. If this does happen, speak to a trusted adult.

FROM GIRLS TO WOMEN

Girls usually go through puberty at a slightly younger age than boys, usually between the ages of 10 and 13, but everyone is different.

When a girl goes through puberty, it means her body is growing into a woman. Her body grows taller and starts to look curvy, with developing breasts and rounded hips. She is slowly becoming an adult.

Changes

One of the first signs of puberty in a girl is when her breasts begin to grow. Then the parts of her body that will make it possible for her to have a baby, called the reproductive system, start getting ready to do their job. Every month, hormones cause one of her ovaries to release a tiny egg into a fallopian tube. The egg moves through the tube to her womb (or uterus).

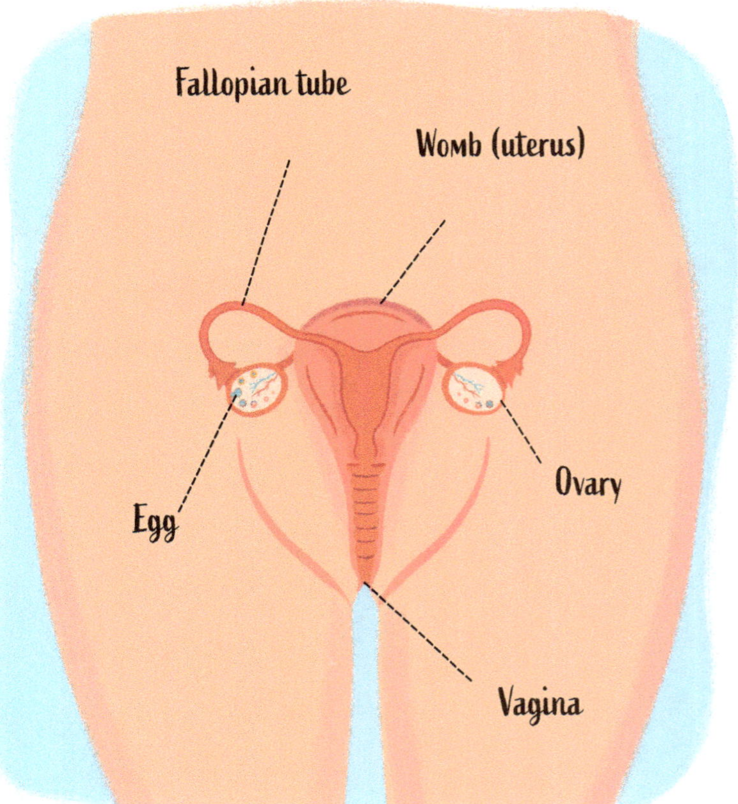

This diagram shows the female reproductive system.

Monthly Period

Usually the tiny egg, along with the lining of the womb, comes out as blood through a girl's vagina. The blood lasts for a few days and is called her monthly period. A pregnant woman won't get her monthly period because the egg stays in the womb and starts to grow into a baby. The womb lining helps the baby grow.

Wearing some sort of sanitary pad, tampon, or menstrual cup soaks up or collects blood when you have your period. You need to change or empty them three or four times a day.

Abi and her friends are teenagers. Even though it's possible for them to become pregnant now, they know that they are not ready to be moms yet.

FROM BOYS TO MEN

When a boy goes through puberty, it means his body is growing into a man. For boys, it usually starts between the ages of 11 and 14. The body grows taller and becomes more muscular. The boy is becoming an adult.

Changes

During puberty, a boy's shoulders and chest get wider. He starts growing hair on his chest, underarms, and between his legs. On his face, he starts growing hair, which he may want to shave.

During puberty, a boy's voice box grows, making his voice deeper. The voice box can be seen as a bump in the neck, called an Adam's apple.

Alex has noticed that his skin is more greasy than it used to be, and he is annoyed when he gets pimples.

Making Sperm

The male reproductive system has a penis and two testicles. The testicles are inside a bag of skin called the scrotum. During puberty, a boy's hormones cause his testicles to start making millions and millions of sperm, getting his body ready for him to be able to father a child with a woman. When millions of tiny sperm flow from the testicles and out through the penis, it is called an ejaculation.

This diagram shows the male reproductive system.

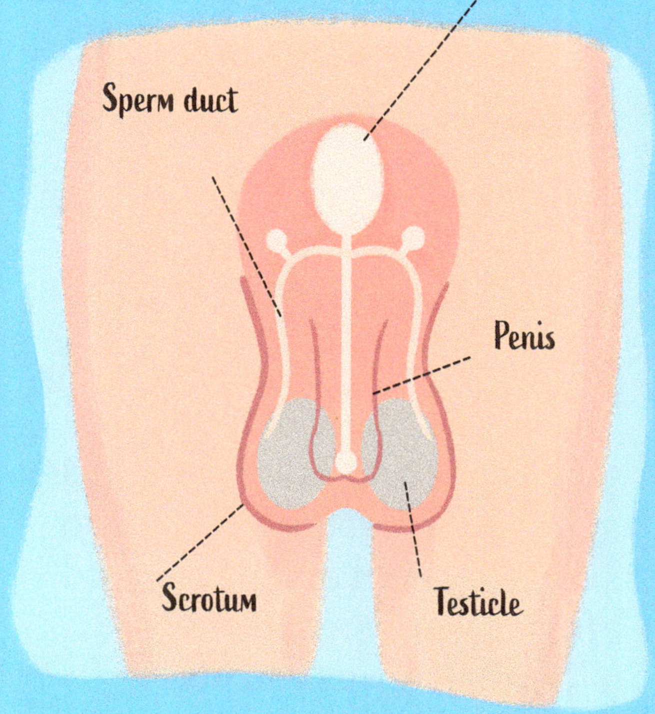

A. J. and his friends spend a lot of time together. One day some of them will want to become dads, but they are not ready for it yet.

LOOKING AFTER YOURSELF

As you grow, it is important to look after your body and your mind. You can do this in several different ways.

Healthy Diet

For your body to work properly, it needs a range of foods that give your body all that it needs. That means eating a balanced diet–the right amount of food from the different food groups. This plate gives you ideas of how to do that.

Active Lifestyle

As well as eating a healthy diet, you need to give your body plenty of exercise to keep it fit and healthy. Running about, swimming, climbing, cycling–all these activities and many others make your heart and lungs work harder and your body stronger.

Rest

Exercising will help you sleep. Sleep is very important since it is the time when your body repairs itself and when your brain stores memories and skills you learned during the day.

When you are asleep, your brain cells build new or stronger connections with other parts of the brain and get rid of unwanted connections. This is how you remember the new skills or information that you learned that day.

Well-Being

It is important to take care of your mental well-being. Happy, sad, upset, worried– all these feelings are normal. If you are worried or sad and these feelings aren't going away, talk to a trusted adult.

Some tips on how to keep well are to talk about your feelings with friends or trusted adults, spend time outdoors, focus on an activity you enjoy, think about happy times, and relax. Helping others helps your own well-being.

Jacob helps his grandmother in the garden once a month. He likes to chat with her about how he is feeling.

AN ADULT

You will become an adult when your body stops growing, probably between the ages of 18 and 25. By then you will feel more independent from your parents or caregivers–and more aware of your own personality.

What do you think you'll do when you're an adult? Will you be an artist, vet, or teacher? Will you travel?

Choices

Being an adult can bring some big decisions. Where will you live? Will you travel? What kind of work will you do? Will you get married? You'll have to decide what's right for you and sometimes you'll make mistakes. Mostly, you'll find a way through any difficulties as life is about learning, even for adults.

Responsibilities

Along with choices, there are responsibilities. You'll need to work to pay for things such as a home. Like children, adults also need plenty of exercise and sleep, and they need to eat a healthy diet. Behaving like an adult means being sensible, while still having fun! Sometimes adults find this hard.

Having Children

Being a mom or dad is one of the biggest responsibilities there is. If you have children, they will depend on you and it will be your job to care for them until they are able to care for themselves.

Being a parent is a lot of fun, but it is not easy.

End of Life

As you get older and older, your hair will turn gray and your skin will get wrinkly. Parts of your body may start to wear out. Keeping active helps many people stay healthy into old age. However, everyone must die sometime. People die and others are born—that is the human life cycle.

Linda and her friends are in their seventies, but they still meet up to go swimming and have fun.

BEING YOU

How you look on the outside is just one small part of who you are. It's what's on the inside that makes you special—your personality—that is, the type of person you are: loud or quiet, careful or risk-taker, what is important to you, your skills and talents, and the way you behave toward other people and situations.

Georgina and her friends may not be pop stars, but they enjoy trying out new dance moves.

Learning All the Time

As you grow up, you'll have the chance to try new things and discover more about yourself. Your body may stop getting taller when you become an adult, but you never stop growing and changing as a person. Your brain continues to develop and learn all through your life as you experience new challenges. So you are always changing, even if those changes can't be seen.

Your Life

Although you've grown up a lot since you were a baby, you're still near the beginning of your life cycle. You've got most of your life ahead of you. You have lots of choices to make. Try to take opportunities when they are in front of you. Some choices will work out well and others maybe not so well. But remember, your life is special. Enjoy it!

Olivia and her friends think that we all need to take better care of planet Earth and the environment before it is too late.

?

What's important to you? The environment? Pets? Family? Friends? Music? Books?

THINGS TO TALK ABOUT AND DO

Growing and Changing

When you are a child, your body is growing and changing. It happens slowly, but suddenly your shoes are too tight or your pants are too short! Talk about the ways you can support your body while it grows and changes.

Think and Talk

Who Is a Trusted Adult?
Talk about adults you trust and why you trust them. Sometimes the hormones that help your body grow and change make you feel moody or upset. If you are feeling upset or worried, tell a trusted adult and talk your worries through with them.

A New Game
Invent a new game involving a ball and people running around. What will you call it? What are the rules? Give it a go!

The Power of YET
Talk about the things you have learned to do since you were born. For instance, you learned to move around and talk when you were still very young. What have you learned to do recently? Sometimes we find things difficult. Maybe you can't swim or ride a bike YET but keep trying and practicing, and you'll be able to one day.

Write

Move More

Write a list of all the sports and activities that you can think of, including hobbies like dancing and skateboarding. How many of them have you tried? Which ones might you like to try soon?

Snack Swap

You can help your body by eating healthy snacks. Write down some snacks and come up with some ideas for snack swaps, such as these:

chocolate cookie	**swap for**	**granola bar**
potato chips	**swap for**	**pita chips**
soda pop	**swap for**	**water**

Record Your Heartbeat

Your pulse is a measure of how fast your heart is pumping blood around your body. Find your pulse by pressing your first two fingers on the underside of your wrist, below your thumb. Using a clock or watch, record your pulse for a minute. Now run around and take your pulse again.

Test Your Memory

Pair up with a friend. Study these words for a minute.

bird	**cup**	**carrot**	**baby**	**pebble**
cat	**table**	**banana**	**tree**	**book**

Now close the book and see how many you can remember. If you are doing this activity alone, write the words down. How many words did you remember?

Create

Paper Plate Art

Look at this illustration of the main food groups. Now choose foods that you like eating from each food group and draw them onto a paper plate to make a healthy meal. Use paint or markers to add color.

GLOSSARY

adult A fully grown person.

cartilage A body tissue that is more bendy than bone but does not stretch.

cell One of the tiny building blocks that make up living things.

control To have power over something in order to deal with it.

diet The food and drink that you normally eat and drink.

energy The power to carry out activities.

environment The natural world in which all plants and animals, including humans, live.

fallopian tube One of the two tubes in a female animal along which eggs pass from the ovaries to the womb (uterus).

food groups The main food groups that make up a balanced diet.

hormone A natural chemical made by the body and released into blood which triggers a reaction. During puberty, hormones trigger the development of the reproductive system.

life cycle Changes that happen through the life of a living thing.

lungs The organs that humans and other animals use for breathing.

menstrual cup A reusable silicone cup inserted into the vagina to collect blood during a period.

mental Connected with what is happening in the mind.

milestones Important stages in growing up.

organ A large body structure with a special function, such as the heart, brain, stomach, or liver.

ovary In an animal, the part of the body that produces eggs.

period The regular (usually monthly) flow of blood experienced by girls and women after puberty when the womb lining breaks down and is released from the body.

personality A set of qualities that make one person different from another.

pregnancy The growth of a baby from an egg and a sperm inside the mother's womb. It lasts roughly 40 weeks.

puberty A stage of the life cycle in which a person begins to grow into an adult.

reproductive system The parts of the body that make it possible to have a baby.

responsibilities Things that a person is trusted to look after.

responsible Able to be trusted; sensible and mature.

romantic Having to do with love.

sperm A male sex cell produced in the testicles.

tantrum Showing bad temper, often by kicking and screaming.

unique The only one of its kind.

uterus The body organ where babies develop before they are born.

vagina A passage that leads to the womb in girls and women.

well-being General happiness and health.

womb The body organ where babies develop before they are born.

TRUSTED ADULTS

Throughout this book, the author advises you to talk to a trusted adult if you are upset, afraid, or confused about something that is going on in your family life. A trusted adult is someone you are happy to be around and who listens to what you say, or someone who has helped you before. It can be many people including your teacher, a teacher's aide, a nurse, your parents, an older sibling, or your grandparents. Not all adults are trusted adults.

FURTHER INFORMATION

WEBSITES

Kids and Exercise
Find out more about the benefits of moving your body.
kidshealth.org/en/parents/exercise.html

How the Body Works
This site has many fun and educational videos for kids like you.
kidshealth.org/en/kids/center/htbw-main-page.html

MyPlate
Learn what the U.S. government has to say about the food groups.
www.myplate.gov/

Puberty and Growing Up
Do you have more questions about the process of growing up? Check out these links.
kidshealth.org/en/kids/grow/

BOOKS

Huddleston, Emma. *Looking Inside the Human Body.* Mankato, MN: The Child's World, 2020.

Miller, Marie-Therese. *Feelings Like Mine.* Minneapolis, MN: Lerner Publications, 2021.

Payne, Kev. *Human Body.* New York, NY: DK, 2021.

Publisher's note to parents and teachers: Our editors have reviewed the websites listed here to make sure they're suitable for students. However, websites may change frequently. Please note that students should always be supervised when they access the internet.

INDEX